Kunda Crawford, Perth.

THE
COUNTRY DIARY
COMPANION

THE
COUNTRY DIARY
COMPANION

JOSEPHINE POOLE · Photographs by SIMON McBRIDE

Book Club Associates
London

This edition published 1984 by Book Club Associates

By arrangement with

Webb & Bower (Publishers) Limited
9 Colleton Crescent, Exeter, Devon EX2 4BY

Designed by Peter Wrigley

This publication is based on the television series
The Country Diary of an Edwardian Lady produced by
Central Independent Television plc.

We would like to thank Rowena Stott, Edith Holden's
great-niece and the owner of the original work, who
has made this publication possible.

Printed and bound in Italy by Arnoldo Mondadori Editore

Typeset in Great Britain by Busby's Typesetting and Design,
Exeter, England

EDITH
HOLDEN

Contents

page

PART I

The Story of Edith Holden

THE FIELDS BEHIND LAPWORTH, with the church spire in the background.

The year 1871 had been cold and wet. August was fine, however, and by September those Victorian ladies who followed the fashion were choosing white or grey for their holiday toilettes. At Balmoral, Queen Victoria was indisposed with rheumatic pains and an infected hand, and after a disturbed night on September 25th, she spent a quiet day. In Birmingham, the booming centre of Midland iron, steel and coal, the annual Onion Fair was over. The Free Christian Society was looking forward to its Grand Bazaar in the Masonic Hall at the end of the week, while Victor Hugo's romance, *The Legend of Notre Dame*, was playing at the Theatre Royal. On this day, Tuesday the 26th September, the feast of St Cyprian the Magician, a baby girl was born whose name, Edith Holden, was to become a household word.

She was christened Edith Blackwell—Blackwell being a family name. She was the fourth of seven children, whose parents had moved from Bristol to Birmingham in 1865. Arthur, her father, was a talented, ambitious, energetic man. His tastes were literary and artistic, but he chose a more practical way of supporting his growing family, and established a paint and varnish business in Bradford Street. Emma, his wife (née Wearing) had been a governess.

At the time of Edith's birth, the Holdens were living at Holly Green house, in Church Road,

SOME OF THE HOLDEN FAMILY WITH FRIENDS— a photograph taken in the late 1890s. Back row, from left: Arthur Matthison, Kenneth Holden, Winnie (centre) and Evelyn (far right). Front row: Arthur Holden (centre), Edith (next right) and Edith Matthison (far right).

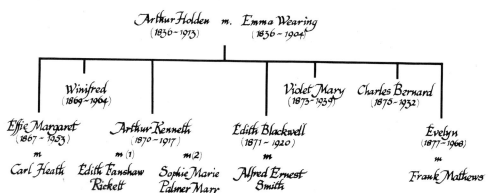

Moseley. They already had two little daughters, Effie Margaret and Winifred, and a boy of a year, Arthur Kenneth. Edith was followed two years later by Violet Mary; then came Charles Bernard in 1875. At this point they moved to a larger house in Acocks Green. In 1877 another daughter, Evelyn, was born, and the family was complete.

Emma Holden had produced seven babies in twelve years, and she remained in poor health for the rest of her life. She engaged a nurse for the children, a local girl called Rosamiah Gazey, who became a pillar of the Holden household. All the children loved her, and she was particularly devoted to Evelyn, who was delicate.

ARTHUR HOLDEN AGED ABOUT THIRTY-FIVE.

The little Holdens were taught by their mother, and from her they learnt first of all to appreciate literature. The house was full of books, from the novels of Sir Walter Scott to the poems of Jean Ingelow. Emma loved to read aloud, and verses the children knew by heart were proudly recited to their father when he came home from work. Later on, the girls studied French and German, and sketching as a matter of course. It was a safe and happy time. Rosamiah and the servants kept things running smoothly for the children, even when their mother was ill, and the family business prospered.

Arthur Holden was a Unitarian, a member of the Birmingham Labour Church. For him, religion and politics were not simply vote-catchers, rungs in the ladder to power. He was genuinely anxious to improve the grim conditions of working men. As soon as he arrived in Birmingham, he took an active part in public life, and was elected to the Town Council in 1873, when he was described in the *Birmingham Morning News* as 'a modest but able and intelligent councillor possessing literary ability of no mean order'. He was a founder member of the Central Literary Association, and subscribed to the Royal Birmingham Society of Artists.

Although he was obliged to work in the city, Arthur loved the countryside. One of his children's greatest joys was to go for a walk with him, for he knew the names of wild flowers and birds. If Emma was too poorly to go with them, they picked bunches of flowers to take home to her, so that she could share in their pleasure.

By 1880 the brick and mortar tentacles of Birmingham were stretching dangerously close to Acocks Green. The Holdens retreated, to Darley Green in Packwood, fifteen miles south of the city. Troutbeck was a new, semi-detached house with a pretty garden bounded by a stream. Like all the Holden houses, it was chosen partly for the convenience of public transport, in this case the railway station. Trains were quicker and cheaper than horses, and businessmen relied on them as a link between home and city.

Kenneth and Bernard naturally took the lion's share of their father's attention. He was, after all, a Victorian, and on them depended the future of the family business. But he was very proud of his gifted daughters. Effie, the eldest, had inherited his own literary talent—later on she would publish her poems. Winnie was the practical one. Slightly built, with a congenital back deformity, she was to be her mother's housekeeper and

THE GARDENS AT PACKWOOD HOUSE.

closest companion. Edith and Violet already showed marked artistic ability, while little Evelyn, the baby of the family, was expected to outshine them all.

Edith was nine when they went to Darley Green. The move was of tremendous importance to her. How excitedly she must have explored her new terrain! There was an old mill with a pond, and at Packwood there was a forge. Sometimes she walked with her mother and sisters in the grounds of Packwood House. The 'house' was more of a mansion, and its elaborate gardens included a fishpond which fascinated her. If they followed the path along the stream at the bottom of the garden, they came to Packwood Hall. This ancient building appealed strongly to little Edith's romantic imagination, but most of all she loved to watch the animals grazing in the fields, or working the farm land. The mechanization of farming had hardly begun, and they were an endless source of wonder and amusement.

No artist entirely outgrows his childhood. Until her marriage, Edith was to return constantly to these happy scenes. She was touchingly attached to them.

Her brothers were going to school by this time. An aunt in Bristol, worried about Emma's health, offered to help by taking in one of the girls, and Effie went to live with her. Now Edith was thirteen, and determined to make a change in her

Peacock
Butterfly

10

own life. She had set her heart on going to the Art School in Birmingham for professional tuition.

The Private Painting and Drawing Society had been founded in Birmingham in 1821. As time passed, it developed into an art school, and it was taken over by the Council in 1845, when the name was changed to the Municipal School of Art. It moved into new buildings in Margaret Street in May, 1884.

Nest and eggs of Blackbird.

Edith came here for classes on three mornings a week. She worked very hard. She was not brilliant, but she made the most of her talent. All pupils were required to pass an examination in model and freehand, or imaginative, drawing within the first two years. Edith won an 'excellent', and a prize, in her freehand examination the following April.

The work of William Morris was closely connected with the school. Founder of the Arts and Crafts Movement, he believed that while men could be brutalized by slum conditions, they could equally be ennobled by beauty, and his designs for textiles, stained glass, wallpapers, books and so on were intended for the beautification of ordinary domestic life. The Arts and Crafts Movement became a popular crusade. It was allied to Socialism, for Morris taught that men could be happy only if they enjoyed their work, and that their production could be good only if they were happy.

No humane person could enjoy the benefits of the industrial revolution, without being disturbed by the conditions of the majority of working people. There were many benevolent societies, both within and outside the church. At the Birmingham Labour Church in Hurst Street, a Socialist spoke every week at the Sunday evening service. The Holdens were usually present, and the girls would bring bunches of flowers from their country garden, for distribution among the sick and poor. The Holden children naturally joined in their parents' socialist-inspired activities, and one of these was the annual works picnic, a day in the country enjoyed by all who worked for Arthur Holden, from the managing director himself to the office boy.

Emma was a Unitarian, like her husband. She was also drawn to spiritualism, and came to believe in her own psychic powers, and in messages received from 'the other side' through automatic writing. Arthur grew to share her

'AMONG THE OAKS' (*left*), an example of Edith's work while a student at the Municipal School of Art in Birmingham.

ONE OF THE WARWICKSHIRE CANALS (*opposite*), a characteristic part of the landscape from which Edith drew much of her inspiration.

conviction, to the point of writing an essay on thought transference, which appeared in the *Central Literary Magazine*. Seances were held at home, to which close friends were invited. Not all the children took part: Evelyn for one would have nothing to do with it. But Edith was susceptible, and believed herself guided by a spirit named Hope.

Kenneth had started work in the family firm of Arthur Holden & Sons, and Violet and Evelyn were pressing their parents to let them join Edith at the Municipal School. In 1890 the family moved again. Gowan Bank was a handsome old house in Kingswood, some sixteen miles from Birmingham. The gardens were large, and included a detached staff cottage. Kingswood station was conveniently near, indeed the railway cutting actually bounded the garden. It was a substantial property, befitting a man of substance.

That autumn Edith had her first public success. One of her pictures, an oil painting called 'A Cosy Quartette', was accepted for exhibition by the Royal Birmingham Society of Artists. The whole family attended the Private View.

She was now nineteen. A model pupil, attentive and conscientious, she worked in talented company. Several of her fellow-students became notable illustrators, and her examiners included Walter Crane. The Municipal School had an excellent reputation, many of its pupils winning awards in national as well as local competitions. Had she lived in London or even Paris, she could hardly have found for herself a better training.

Next summer she finished her basic studies, and it was time to specialize. For her, the choice was easy. She had inherited her mother's deep love of nature—birds, animals and plants. She decided to concentrate on animal painting, and her tutors recommended the artist and teacher, Joseph Denovan Adam. He worked at Craigmill, just outside Stirling in Scotland. Here he had set up

stables and paddocks for horses and donkeys, cattle and sheep, so that his students—up to twenty-five at a time—could observe and draw them in natural surroundings. He had even built a studio with glass sides, so that work could go on when it rained.

Most of the students lived in lodgings, but a few stayed at Craigmill with Denovan, his wife and children. Edith was one of these. She left home in August, 1891, accompanied by her father. No doubt she was nervous at the prospect of going out into the world, and sorry to say good-bye to her family, but she must have found home irksome in some ways, centred as it had to be on her sick mother, and perhaps she was glad to escape from inevitable comparison with her two extremely talented younger sisters.

Opposite and below:
From
The Country Diary of an Edwardian Lady

Fine·leaved Heath.
(Erica cinerea)

From the first, she loved Craigmill. She would have found it more difficult to settle in without the young Adam children, for she was a quiet, reserved girl. But one of the boys, also called Denovan, had been ill for some time, and she made a pet of him. She loved the animals roaming in the park, and learnt from the artist how to approach them without fear. Then the grandeur and romance of the setting, with its ancient castle and abbey, its fir woods and river, fired her artistic imagination. Her work improved enormously in these surroundings, and in her spare time she was an indefatigable sightseer.

She stayed for a year in Scotland. Creatively

speaking, she was to remain deeply influenced by the experience, which would dictate many of her exhibition pictures for years to come.

Meanwhile her eldest sister Effie had gone to Sweden to study the Arts and Crafts Movement there, while Evelyn had joined Violet at the Municipal School. Both girls were brilliant students, bolder and more self-confident than Edith had been. Evelyn was only fourteen when she won a prize for a design in stained glass, and while still teenagers they were making a reputation as illustrators. Sometimes they worked together. The Birmingham School of Book Decorators not only made designs, but cut blocks, and could even print books. Such A to Z production was in the true spirit of the Movement, and won the personal praise of William Morris.

Much entertaining was done at Gowan Bank. Visiting lecturers in socialism or spiritualism were always invited there, not forgetting the Sunday evening preacher at the Labour church. There were literary discussions, poetry recitals, musical evenings, and amateur dramatics in the garden, or the old chapel if it rained. Kenneth Holden was a particularly enthusiastic member of the little drama company which had been founded by Arthur Matthison, a young man who had joined the family business.

Others came with nothing but poverty to recommend them. The Birmingham Labour Church had begun a series of evening meetings to get children out of the slums. The Cinderella Club, as it was called, offered food, prayers and fairy stories. It flourished. A Christmas party and summer outings, including one to Gowan Bank, were organized, and in 1896 Arthur Holden lent his staff cottage for April, May and June, so that thirty-five sick children each had a fortnight's holiday there, to their immeasurable happiness and improvement.

Gowan Bank was an ideal home in many ways, but it was large and expensive, and it became more of a worry than a pleasure to the elderly parents. Emma's health had deteriorated until she had to spend most of her time lying down. In 1897 Arthur moved his family to Dorridge, to a smaller modern house called Woodside. They

Orange-tip Butterfly
(Euchloe Cardimines)

Oxe-eye Daisy
(Chrysanthemum leucanthemum)

Purple Clover
(Trifolium pratense)

White or Dutch Clover
(Trifolium rèpans)

Meadow Fox-Tail Grass
(Alopecurus pratensis)

MRS ANNE TRATHEN, who kept the post office at Dousland in Dartmoor, with her daughter Belle and her son Carol.

EVELYN, the youngest of the Holden sisters, who married Frank Mathews, a local philanthropist.

knew that part of the country already. It was several miles from Birmingham, but Knowle Station was close, and the house was prettily situated on the edge of Dorridge Wood.

Winnie was housekeeper now, and devoted herself to her mother. They had much in common. She sat beside her, reading aloud, or quietly sketching in the garden. Emma's involvement in spiritualism increased as her health declined. She was considered a particularly responsive medium, and Winnie joined her in automatic writing.

Edith was working hard, painting and modelling animals. Lacking Highland cattle, her subjects were horses and dogs, and in addition she produced four pictures a year to exhibit in Birmingham. But Scotland was still her favourite subject, and after the death of Denovan Adam she went there regularly to stay with his widow. She called these visits holidays, but in fact they were times of intense activity. It was as if she had to store all her impressions on paper and canvas, to feed her inspiration until she came north again.

She decided to visit Dartmoor in the spring of 1902. As usual she took her painting equipment. There was a train service direct from Birmingham to Plymouth, and she spent a night with her aunt near Bristol on the way. From Plymouth she took a local train to Dousland, a little village near Princetown, deep in the wild beauty of the moor. She stayed at The Grange, which boasted tennis courts and a ballroom—implying a steady flow of summer visitors.

Edith Holden
at her easel.

THE RIVER PLYM as it flows through the wooded valleys of south-west Dartmoor.

This was to be the first of many visits over the next eight years. She fell in love with the place, and friendships followed. Dousland Post Office was kept by Mrs Trathen, the wife of a stone mason. Her five teenage children, two girls and three boys, accompanied Edith on her expeditions. An uncritical audience, they marvelled at her sketches, and laughed at her comic drawings and rhymes. She enjoyed her position in the lively group. She was fond of them all, but she was particularly attached to Belle

Wood Spurge
(Euphorbia amygdaloides)

SMALL CAPS Sheepstor and Burrator in the moors above Dousland where Edith spent many holidays with the Trathens.

Trathen. That friendship with the pretty, unspoilt country girl became very precious to her.

For at home, the closely-knit family circle was breaking up. Effie had married in 1900. Her husband, Carl Heath, was a professional teacher, an intellectual Socialist whom she met in Sweden. Now, two years later, Evelyn became engaged to Frank Mathews. He was a regular visitor at Woodside, and one of the people most involved in the Cinderella Club. In 1897 he had founded the Hurst Street Mission, specifically to care for the

convalescence of sick and crippled children. All the Holden girls had inherited their father's concern for the unfortunate, and this was a quality they looked for, and loved, in their friends, Frank and Evelyn were married in 1904, and took away with them Rosamiah Gazey who had lived faithfully with the family for so many years.

Evelyn's wedding was a quiet occasion, for her mother was seriously ill. She died three months later. But Arthur and his remaining daughters did not feel this as a total separation, for they were convinced that she kept in touch with them through Winnie's automatic writing. This year Violet began teaching at the Municipal School of Art.

Besides his bereavement, poor Arthur had financial difficulties to trouble him. Arthur Holden & Sons had become a limited company to raise the capital needed to keep pace with growing competition. Now the outside shareholders were pressing for a Board of Control, because they felt that the founder of the company was too old to manage it. Kenneth stood by his father, but Bernard, the younger brother, and Arthur Matthison opposed him. The loyalties of the sisters were painfully divided. By taking her father's part, Edith found herself in conflict with Violet and Evelyn. It was an unhappy situation, and to make matters worse, the company's financial situation did not improve. Once more, Arthur sought a smaller house for his family.

They moved to Olton in 1905. The new house was in Kineton Green Road, and they called it, nostalgically, Gowan Bank. Kenneth and Bernard had left home, and there were only three girls left—Winifred, Edith and Violet. They employed a resident cook-housekeeper, two women who came in by the day to clean and do the laundry, and a gardener twice a week. Olton was closer to Birmingham, and fast developing into a commuter village, but there were lanes and fields, and Edith was still within cycling distance of her beloved childhood scenes.

Soon after the move, she made an important new friendship. Miss Burd, the sister of the vicar of Shirley, kept a small private school for girls in Solihull, and early in 1906 Edith agreed to teach drawing there on Friday afternoons. It was an old-fashioned establishment with strict discipline, and, for the time, an unusual emphasis on sport, including cricket. Edith was to teach the older girls, aged from fourteen to seventeen. They were already working on a project, diaries intended to record, with sketches and literary quotations, the

A Postcard by Edith Holden (*left*) for the Royal Society for the Prevention of Cruelty to Animals.

The Landscape around Callander (*right*), in the foothills of the Trossachs in Scotland.

One of her Drawings (*opposite above*) from the children's book, *Animals Around Us*.

changing of the seasons. Edith decided to link these with her lessons. Every week she brought specimens of plants for the current month, carefully wrapped, and carried to school in her bicycle basket. She kept a diary of *Nature Notes* herself, to encourage her class.

She wasn't adored, as some art teachers are by their adolescent pupils. But the girls grew to respect her. Her standards were high, because she herself had been a model student. She didn't look for brilliance, she simply required each girl to do her best, and she never despised work that was carefully done. Her results were good, and some of her pupils were in fact very promising.

She went to Dartmoor for Easter, 1906, and amused herself with painting portraits of a pony mare and foal belonging to the Trathens. Her oil painting, 'Study of Chaffinch's Nest and Hawthorns', which she exhibited later, derived from this particular holiday, for in her *Nature Notes* she recorded finding such a nest nearly finished on Easter Sunday.

The following August she returned to Scotland. Mrs Adam was running a small boarding house near the Trossachs, and Edith had a wonderful time. The weather was atrocious, but she managed to explore the hills and lakes on foot, by bicycle and boat, filling her sketchbook with ideas and observations. The country was rich in history, part fact, part legend, darkly romantic tales she knew already from the novels of Sir Walter Scott. She visited Oban, travelling on the spectacular West Highland Railway from Callander, before returning to Craigmill to meet

85.

Fox-glove (Digitalis purpurea)
Trailing Rose (Rosa arvensis)

HUCKWORTHY BRIDGE ON DARTMOOR (*above*), the scene of Edith Holden's oil painting (*right*), which she gave to Belle Trathen as a wedding present.

again many people she had known in her student days. Young Denovan Adam was a successful artist by this time, but he welcomed the girl who had been so kind to him when he was a sickly boy.

She came home in time for her birthday. Thirty-five years had passed since she first opened her eyes on the world whose small beauties she was to depict with such a loving hand. 1906 drew to an end, and closing her diary she put it away, without imagining that it was of interest to anyone. It was to lie undiscovered for seventy years.

Edith was closest to Effie of all her sisters, and she found Carl Heath equally sympathetic. Effie and Carl lived in London, and were actively involved in the work of various societies, all of a humanitarian and socialist nature. Edith visited them often, and when she was at home she sorely missed the stimulation of London life, the plans and opinions of the Heaths and their friends. In the spring of 1907 she exhibited in Birmingham for the last time. Her painting was called 'A Moorland Pasture', and it was based on studies of Highland cattle she had made the previous summer in Scotland. She already planned to offer another of her Scottish pictures, 'The Rowan Tree', for the Royal Academy Summer Exhibition in London.

She was becoming known for her animal drawing. Early that year she produced an illustrated calendar, one page of which appeared each month in the magazine *The Animals' Friend*, published by the National Council for Animal Welfare. The complete calendar was on sale at Christmas, in aid of the charity. The RSPCA commissioned her to design postcards, and in the autumn she worked on a book with Effie. It was a little book, the right size for a child's hands, called *Birds, Beasts and Fishes*, and it included animal poems for children with decorations by Edith. Besides all these projects, she was still teaching at the Solihull School for Girls, and she found time to holiday on Dartmoor. This year, she stayed with the Trathens.

Now that her work was reaching a wider public, the Walker Gallery in Liverpool accepted two of her paintings, while another was taken by the Society of Women Artists. She spent the summer holidays of 1908 in London. Carl and Effie were in France, but by this time she had

friends of her own in the city. One of them was Ernest Smith, a sculptor seven years younger than herself. No one expected Edith to blossom into romance. There was no reason to discuss her growing friendship with Ernest, and she kept it to herself. Belle Trathen was married that August, and Edith sent her an oil painting of Huckworthy Bridge on Dartmoor, a beauty spot that had happy memories for them both.

At home, life for the sisters was complicated by the financial troubles of the family firm, and saddened by anxiety for their father who was old and ill. Edith spent several weeks in London in the summer of 1909. This was partly a business trip, and it resulted in several commissions. No matter how trivial the work, if she accepted it she could be relied on to do it to the best of her ability. She never produced a careless drawing, and it was not surprising that her reputation grew.

She resigned her post at the Solihull School for Girls in 1910. On June 1st, 1911, she walked into Chelsea Register Office on the arm of Alfred Ernest Smith, and they were married by special licence.

Ernest had been a pupil of the sculptor and professor Lanteri, at the Royal College of Art. Lanteri thought highly of him, and he had graduated to pupil-teacher at the college. The fashionable sculptress, the Countess Feodora

AN EXAMPLE OF EDITH'S ILLUSTRATIONS for *The Animals' Friend*, the magazine of the National Council for Animals' Welfare.

EDITH at about the time of her marriage.

Gleichen, saw his work and engaged him as her principal assistant. Her studio was in St James's Palace, and here Edith met many of the most distinguished artists of the day, including Sir George Frampton, the sculptor of Peter Pan in Kensington Gardens. But she wisely pursued her own career, and exhibited once more at the Royal Academy in 1917.

They lived in Chelsea, in a flat in Oakley Crescent. Ernest had a brother, Frederick, who taught at the Wolverhampton School of Art. He was an artist and craftsman, and now that she lived in London, Edith did her best to promote his work. Arthur Holden died in 1913, an old man of seventy-seven. Carol Trathen, who she had known from a boy, and to whom she had taught French by correspondence, fought and was killed in the First World War. Fond as she was of all the Trathens, this was a bitter blow.

She suffered from recurrent headaches, so severe sometimes that they made her giddy. When she woke on the morning of March 15th, 1920, the pain was bad, and Ernest advised her to take a walk later on, as he thought the exercise would do her good. Friends were coming for Easter, and they discussed this at breakfast. Edith was looking forward to the visit. Then Ernest left for the studio in St James's, and later Edith took his advice and went out for a walk by the river. The University crews were practising for the boat race, and it amused her to watch them. It was an early spring day of sunshine and showers. She was warmly dressed, and took her umbrella.

When Ernest came home, she was still out, though the table was laid for supper. He assumed she had made last-minute plans to see friends or go to the theatre, though that would have been out of character, and she had left no note. There was no message from her at the studio next morning. This made him anxious. He hurried home, and on his return met a policeman, who told him that she was dead.

A constable on duty near Kew Gardens Walk, early on Tuesday morning, had seen the body of a woman lying face downwards in the backwater of the Thames. A rolled umbrella floated beside her. At the water's edge lay a bunch of chestnut buds, and examination showed that one of these had snapped off the bough of a tree overhanging the river. Evidently Edith had tried to reach the branch with the crook of her umbrella, and stretching out just too far, she had lost her balance, and fallen into the water.

At the inquest, Ernest confirmed that his wife was subject to neuralgia, and that she suffered from dizzy fits when she had a headache. He agreed that she often brought home buds and flowers to draw. The Richmond Coroner recorded a verdict of 'Found Drowned'.

Her family was horrified by the tragedy. She had lost touch with them to some extent after her marriage, and the question was raised, whether she had committed suicide. But her friends were certain that it had been an accident. Frederick's wife Dorothy, in particular, had often discussed her spiritualist and religious beliefs with Edith, and knew how strongly she condemned self-destruction. Quite apart from any giddiness and shock, she was wearing heavy clothes so early in the year, and a younger, stronger woman might well have drowned in the same circumstances.

Edith's life had been uneventful, from a worldly point of view. She was quiet, unassuming, a good friend. At a time when many women of her kind led an easy life, she had worked hard, but once her husband and family were dead, there was no reason to think that her memory would be perpetuated—that she would 'come back', as she herself had predicted. But just as the flowers in an old garden spring up when the ground is cleared, so the delicate paintings in the brown diary were destined to survive the chance and change of two generations. Disciple extraordinary of William Morris, how much she was to embellish domesticity! They would flower all over again in countless homes, and give pleasure to more people than she could possibly have imagined.

Above and opposite: From *The Country Diary of an Edwardian Lady*.

ILLUSTRATIONS BY EDITH HOLDEN (*above left and left*) for *Woodland Whisperings*, a collection of poetry for children published in 1911.

'71

June

Willow Warbler
feeding young.

PART II
The Story of the Central Independent Television series

PIPPA GUARD, AS EDITH HOLDEN, with a fledgling blue tit.
It had fallen out of its nest and she cared for it until
it could fly.

ARTHUR AND EMMA HOLDEN had seven children, and even in its most prosperous days, the family was not rich. Emma taught her daughters herself, for she had been a governess, and it was from her that they learnt the rudiments of drawing. Edith's natural talent, early awakened, was to remain a source of deep and lasting pleasure. All her life she liked nothing better than a simple expedition, often by bicycle (*left*), to sketch out of doors, or collect specimens to copy at home.

HAVING ALL THE FAMILY TOGETHER brought back memories of their childhood (*above*). Edith was four years old when the family moved outside Birmingham. The open country was a wonderland to her. Her sister Winnie, the second of the Holden girls, kept a watchful eye over the other children. She could be relied on to remember dry boots and clean handkerchiefs, supervise lessons, and ensure that Evelyn, the baby, didn't catch cold.

EDITH HAD INHERITED a keen sense of beauty, and the invaluable quality of patience to observe. Emma recognized these gifts in her little daughter, and helped her to develop them. To read the *Nature Notes* so many years later is to accompany Edith on a country walk, where nothing is too small to escape notice; when, for example: 'every twig on every tree and bush was outlined in silver tracery against the sky. Some of the dead grasses and seed vessels ... were especially beautiful, every detail of them sparkling with frost crystals in the sunshine ... .'

THE WIND WAS BITTER, but hedging and ditching (*above*) still had to be done by hand. Edith would always be torn between the romance of the old ways—the quiet patience of the worker, whether man or horse, that hardly interrupted the landscape—and her sympathy for him as a person with his thin coat and chilblained fingers.

EDITH WAS THIRTEEN (*right*) when she persuaded her parents to let her study drawing at the Municipal School of Art in Birmingham. The training was thorough, and formal. She was later joined at the School by Violet and Evelyn, and all three sisters won the respect of their teachers, for their work was always faithfully observed and carefully done.

SOMETIMES THE STUDENTS worked outside (*above*), which Edith found very distracting. It was so difficult to concentrate in the open air, when the wind was blowing and the birds singing. But gradually she learnt to approach her subject with the precision of a scientist, as well as the rapture of a poet.

34

ARTHUR HOLDEN made sure that working conditions in his firm were well above average in the city, but society in general was increasingly concerned over the hardships of many workpeople. Worst of all was the plight of slum children (*left*)—their expectations of health and happiness were poor. These two children were fortunate enough to be cared for in Frank Mathews' (a friend of Kenneth's) convalescent home for children at Chadwick End near Birmingham.

THE BIRMINGHAM LABOUR CHURCH, which the Holdens attended, had started a series of evening meetings for the poorest children, providing food, prayers and fairy stories. Arthur Holden took an active interest in the 'Cinderella Club', as it was called, and when he moved to Gowan Bank, a large house in Kingswood, he lent his garden cottage to the Club, so that each child could enjoy a fortnight's holiday in the country. The effects of the Club were transported in a horse-drawn furniture van (*above*). Edith took the opportunity to sketch some of the children—those she could persuade to stand still for a minute!

ONE SNOWY DAY Frank Mathews appeared on the Holdens' doorstep, carrying Rosie Logan. The little girl had measles, and there was no-one to look after her. Edith welcomed her, and nursed her. As Rosie recovered, she became fascinated by life at Gowan Bank—especially Edith's part in it (*above*). It seemed so strange, for instance, to feed the birds, when at home there was little enough for the children to eat! 'There were some terrible battles among the Tits this morning. One tiny Blue-cap took possession of the coconut, sitting down in the middle of it and bidding defiance to all the others. It was very funny to see him squatting in the shell, sparring and hissing at a Great Tit who came at him with open wings and beak.'

ROSIE HAD LIVED all her short life in the city, but even so her total ignorance of country life amazed Edith. She was eager to learn, however, and Edith felt almost as if she was giving sight to the blind. Rosie's greatest treat was to be taken for a walk (*right*). 'The Elm trees are just breaking into blossom and the Willows are showing their downy white catkins—very small as yet.' The daffodils were a blaze of glory now, along the river, and the woods rang with the songs of innumerable birds—'such a chorus of voices from every hedge and tree!'

THE BUDS ON THE HUGE OAKS along Lapworth Lane were still tight, but hazels were boldly opening into green.

Edith soon found that Rosie was taking up most of her time. However one cold spring day she escaped from the house, and bicycled to Packwood. On the way she passed a rookery (*above*). 'The rooks were all very busy building up their old nest, and a great deal of chatter they made over it.' The pupil-teacher relationship was very satisfying to both of them, and Edith was sorry when Mrs Logan came to collect her little daughter, and took her away in a cab.

The garden at Packwood Hall was full of snowdrops. While she was there, the farmer came out with a new-born lamb to show her (*right*). She wrote later: 'I held it in my arms and it seemed quite fearless—poking its little black head up into my face.'

41

E DITH PUT UP HER EASEL in a sheltered corner, and sketched the ploughman (*above*) as he walked slowly behind his horses, turning the rich brown furrow. Later, indoors, she completed her picture in water colours, adding hedge birds on a blackthorn spray, and rooks wheeling over the curve of the field.

L IFE WAS NOT ALL TOIL for the young Holdens, though the boys worked in the family firm, and the girls took their studies and social responsibilities seriously. The large house and garden at Kingswood were ideal for entertainments, including amateur dramatics. Kenneth was particularly involved in these, and Edith was always willing to paint a set (*right*), or act a part.

BRUSHWOOD (*above*) was one of the places Edith visited regularly. There were beds of white violets growing near the ford, and trailing wreaths of white periwinkle. In rough conditions she had to carry her bicycle nearly a quarter of a mile down the steep, muddy track. At the bottom she propped it against the bank, and sat on a fence to eat her picnic. 'A beautiful Jay in all the glory of his spring plumage flew screaming across the lane into a spinney of larch trees opposite. He seemed to resent the intrusion of a human being in such an unfrequented spot.'

E DITH HAD WORKED VERY HARD, observing, drawing, endlessly correcting. Now she had a reward (*above*). The Royal Birmingham Society of Artists had accepted one of her pictures for exhibition. It was an oil painting called 'A Cosy Quartette', and the whole family attended the private view.

T HE CHILDREN of the Cinderella Club (*right*) were not forgotten in the fun and games. Completely unsophisticated, they were easy to please, and expressed their appreciation by cheering loudly, or stamping their boots. A Magic Lantern show was always popular—particularly as it included cocoa and cake.

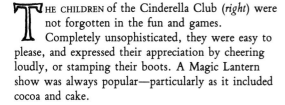

48

BIRMINGHAM WAS SURROUNDED by rich and beautiful country, and it seems horrifying that so many city children pined for want of farm food and fresh air. It is a grim fact that most farm animals (*above left*) were better cared for than the children in the slums.

EDITH GAVE WEEKLY ART CLASSES (*left*) at the Solihull school for girls, teaching the older students on Friday afternoons. They copied fresh flowers into their drawing books, with seasonal literary quotations to point each month. All drawings had to be passed by Edith before she allowed them to be painted, and she insisted on a high standard of workmanship, regardless of talent. The girls progressed from class work to sketching out of doors, and they were encouraged to take their drawing books home with them, to record what they saw out of school hours. Edith did the same, and some of the most charming work in the *Diary* comes from Dartmoor during the Easter holidays.

I T WAS A LONG JOURNEY from Birmingham to Dousland (*above*), the moorland village where Edith spent such happy holidays. She had to change at Plymouth, and take a local train. How eagerly she scanned the moor, as the little train puffed along, stopping at every station! 'Primroses thick all along the line,' she noted in her *Diary*. The pony and trap met her at the station and took her to the Grange, which provided tennis, croquet and even dancing for summer visitors. Edith preferred to stay there out of season, and she looked forward particularly to seeing Belle Trathen, whose mother kept the post office at Dousland. Edith was fond of all the Trathens, and wrote to them regularly from home, but Belle was her favourite.

E DITH SET UP HER EASEL in a field near her hotel, and started to paint Jess and her foal. Great patience, as well as skill was required, but she was very happy out of doors, quietly working in the sunshine. She had been taught how to draw horses and cattle in their natural surroundings, and although Jess shied away at first from the table, chair and easel, Edith's gentle movements and soothing voice reassured her, and soon she took no notice of the unaccustomed artist's furniture.

EDITH WAS A ROMANTIC at heart, and her
imagination was fired by stern landscapes like
Burrator (*above*). Perhaps a fortress once stood
there to defend forgotten boundaries. The great
stone slabs that lay about the moor might have
marked the graves of ancient chiefs. Here the wild
ponies ran as sure-footed as goats, and the
blackthorns were briefly glorious with foamy
blossom. Small birds darted between them and the
gorse bushes, while high above, the larks were
singing their hearts out. Edith noticed how dry the
country was that Easter. She remarked in her *Diary*
that 'a good storm of rain would bring out many
more flowers'.

EDITH WALKED WITH HER FRIENDS along the River Plym. Belle and Robert had eyes only for each other, but Edith looked about her. She wrote later in her *Diary* 'We walked to Plym Bridge. ... A Water Ouzel skimmed across the river and in under the archway of the old stone bridge, every cranny of which was green with tiny ferns.'

Later Edith and Belle shared a picnic (*below*) in the sunshine, near Huckworthy Bridge. The wind was cold, and they needed their warm clothes. Now Belle took Edith into her confidence, and had the joy of describing her lover, while her companion listened attentively, made appreciative comments, and asked all the right questions.

EDITH WAS PAINTING in the hotel grounds, when Belle exclaimed that she saw the 'Adder Man' approaching. She put down her brush, and waited for him with great curiosity. She had heard all about him. Adders were much dreaded by the country people, but he handled them fearlessly. She was glad of this opportunity to meet him. He wore a battered felt hat in all weathers. He brought two snakes from the moor, one of them over two feet long. Edith approached boldly, and later described how he held up one by the scruff and forced open its mouth with a stick, 'to show her the two little pink fangs in the upper jaw' (*above*). She wrote: 'When on the ground they reared themselves up and hissed, and struck repeatedly at a walking stick placed in front of them.' She completed the incident with two paintings, showing the chain of black diamonds and spots along the spine, that distinguishes adders from harmless species.

EDITH WAS ALONE IN THE WOOD above the River Plym, sketching a peacock butterfly. While she worked, she thought about the love between Robert and Belle, that had transformed her friend. Suddenly, Belle appeared as in a dream (*above*), running through the steeply sloping wood. She was dressed all in white, and looked like a bride, or a May Queen. Robert had crowned her with a

wreath of wild flowers, and as Edith watched, he
kissed her. Around them, in the high vaulting of the
trees, the birds sang as if they were in Paradise.

ROBERT AND BELLE TOOK EDITH TO YANNADON
Down (*above*), to watch the sun set behind
the hills. Just as the great glowing orb
touched the earth, a hawk sailed up, up until it hung
high above them in the clear sky. It remained poised
there a minute, quivering like a wind-stroked sail on
a far gold sea; then it dropped, through the false
horizon of purplish clouds, into the shadowy
plantation. Edith, and Belle and Robert hand in
hand, stood watching until the sun dipped out of
sight.

DARTMOOR WAS MAGICAL to Edith—and so was
Scotland (*right*). As a girl she had spent a
year at Craigmill, just outside Stirling,
studying under the artist Joseph Denovan Adam. She
had been very happy in his studio, learning how to
paint animals, and when her course was finished she
continued to visit Scotland regularly.

T o EDITH THE NORTH COUNTRY was an irresistible blend of grandeur and romance. Here she found herself in a different world, one of primitive splendour, passion and beauty. How well she understood the tale of the maiden who cast herself into the waterfall (*above left*) for love, and was borne away drowning on the foaming torrent!

A T FIRST IT HAD SEEMED INSANE to set up her easel on a moor surrounded by cattle (*left*), but she learnt from Denovan Adam how to approach them without fear.

W HEN EDITH WAS NOT DRAWING, she was looking—she was an avid sightseer. She was ready to explore the hills and lochs (*above*) on foot, by bicycle and boat. After Denovan Adam's death she kept in touch with his widow and son, and often stayed with them on her visits.

'GOODBYE TO SCOTLAND and back to the Midlands once more'—she was always sorry to go. The wilderness of moors, dark mountains and reflecting water (*above*) would keep its place in her heart and imagination.

WHEN THE HOLDENS MOVED from Kingswood to Dorridge (*right*), the young people missed the large house, and beautiful garden. But Arthur Holden was anxious to economize, for the family firm was going through a difficult time. He was worried about Emma, too, and hoped that a smaller, more modern house would be less tiring for her. Woodside was within easy distance of Edith's favourite haunts. 'Visited the violet wood this evening; it is quite green and shady there now, as most of the trees are firs and sycamores and the latter are in leaf. The ground was covered with Wild Arums, all in flower ... .'

She went out as usual, collected specimens, and took them home to copy (*right*). Given a table and chair, and enough light to paint by, Edith could feel at home anywhere.

FRANK MATHEWS had been put in charge of Chadwick End, the convalescent home for sick and crippled children. Today they were enjoying a May Day celebration (*right*). Evelyn, youngest of the Holden sisters, joined them in a dance. That May Day was a double celebration for them both, for he had just asked her to marry him.

A WATERCOLOUR by Edith Holden.

THERE WAS NO DOUBT IN EVELYN'S MIND as she stood beside Frank on her wedding day. A beautiful, intelligent and extremely talented young woman, she loved him for his principles, his deep commitment to the under-privileged. If marriage to him meant giving up her very promising career as an artist, she was prepared to do it.

THE TROUBLES AT ARTHUR HOLDEN'S FIRM were
crystallizing into a struggle between his sons,
Kenneth and Bernard. Kenneth was unhappily
married, and perhaps this made him fanatical in his
adherence to his father's old-fashioned, pure socialist
principles, while Bernard was more of a capitalist in
his outlook. The sisters were bound to take sides,
and this was particularly painful for Edith, who
loved her brothers. She went to Stratford to spend a
weekend with Bernard—and found Evelyn there
unexpectedly. The three of them went boating
together (*overleaf*). A perfectly peaceful river
scene—but for Edith it was marred by the intrusion
of family politics.

EVERY SUMMER Arthur Holden and Sons, its directors, managers, and workers down to the smallest office boy, had a day out in the country. Their wives and children went too. The Holden girls were an important part of the festivities, for they provided the picnic. Winnie filled the hampers (*above*), while Edith corrected school notebooks in a corner of the kitchen. For days before, the whole house smelt deliciously of roasts and pies.

WHEN EDITH felt crushed by family pressures, she took refuge in the country (*above*). 'I saw a moorhen's nest today, it was placed on the stump of an old alder tree, at the edge of a pond, just out of reach of the bank ...' She was not too old—she never would be—to thrill to the sight of a newly-born lamb on the farm by Packwood Manor.

THE WORKS OUTING was held in a meadow by the river. There were country entertainments: apple bobbing, skittles, coconut shies; while a band played cheerfully under the cloudless sky. Arthur Holden presided at the head of the table which was draped with a white cloth, and loaded with food and drink. People sat where they liked, the greatest by the least, while Winnie organized the distribution of the feast. It was a great occasion, this year as every year, and if there was friction beneath the surface, no-one would have suspected it. Edith's ideal of family unity appeared complete. A day out in the country meant fishing the river Avon for one boy (*above*), even though his movements were impeded by his best collar and cuffs. All the ladies, even the very young ones, wore hats.

IT WAS DIFFICULT BICYCLING in a long skirt and petticoats (*right*), but Edith was used to it, and thought nothing of an excursion of ten or fifteen miles. She noticed yellow irises in flower among the rushes in the marsh, and 'a beautiful Demoiselle Dragonfly ... skimming across the water'. The trees in full summer foliage made an unbroken arch above her, so that the lane was dark and green.

YARNINGALE COMMON (*above*) seemed an ideal
place for an outing with her students from
Solihull Girls' School. So many different wild
flowers grew there, and there were 'great numbers
of birds, chiefly linnets and warblers'. The girls
would enjoy sketching out of doors.

A HORSE-DRAWN WAGON (*top right*) carried
Edith and her students to Yarningale
Common. The girls wore school uniform,
including tie and boater, and carried their
sketchbooks and paints. They arranged their long
skirts and sat on straw in the bottom of the wagon.
Edith was reserved, but she was not a disciplinarian
like the headmistress, Miss Bird. The girls enjoyed
the holiday, and chattered and joked as they jolted
along, under a cloudless sky.

MANY PEOPLE CROSSED THE COMMON without noticing the tiny flowers that grew there. The girls collected specimens, and settled down in the shade to draw. At midday there was a picnic (*centre right*), simple school food, but delicious eaten in the sunshine. There were many butterflies on the common, particularly Garden Whites and Meadow Browns. Edith noticed how the short grass smelt of thyme, though the plants were not yet in flower.

WHEN THE PICNIC WAS EATEN to the last crumb, and the girls had rested a little, Edith took them to look for birds' nests. They were thrilled to discover eight nests among the gorse and brambles. The eggs had mostly hatched, but in one—a yellowhammer's—they found four. As Edith looked at the tiny eggs (*above*), which she could have crushed with a finger, she was deeply moved. She had a clear vision of the vulnerability, as well as the tenacity of nature.

Not far from Yarningale, new houses were being built. Industry was booming in Birmingham, and those who could afford it were moving out of the centre. The Holdens themselves lived in a new house on the outskirts of the city, but when Edith saw the trees hacked down and burning, and the ground laid waste, she could hardly bear it. She knew that it was odd to feel so, that to most people an elder or bramble bush had no value. To her, even a stinging nettle was an essential part of a whole.

E FFIE, THE ELDEST OF THE HOLDEN GIRLS, had married and lived in London. Edith enjoyed going to visit her, and meeting her friends who seemed much more exciting than the people she knew in Birmingham. Among them was a young man, Ernest Smith, the brilliant pupil of the sculptor Lanteri. When he visited Birmingham, it was Edith's turn to show him the beauties of the countryside (*left*) surrounding the city.

B EYOND WOOTTON, the cupped green hills rose to the summer sky. This pastoral landscape (*below*), with its shady oaks and quietly grazing cattle, was the background to a deepening relationship between Edith and Ernest. Although he was seven years younger, he was irresistibly attracted to her. He admired the careful observation in her drawings, while her reserve made her an intriguing mystery.

ERNEST AND EDITH were out walking together (*left*), when they heard a cuckoo. Edith remembered an old wives' tale: 'If when you hear the cuckoo, you begin to run and count the cuckoo's cries ... you will add as many years to your life as you count calls.' Ernest at once began to run, pulling her after him, and stumbling and laughing they hurried through the barley field. Suddenly she tripped, and would have fallen, but he caught her. How many cries? Neither of them could remember.

NOW THE HOUSE WAS QUIET (*above*), for her father and sisters were already asleep. This was the time to put down her inmost thoughts, but perhaps she never did. Perhaps she simply wrote, remembering her *Diary*: 'June has been a very hot month, with a large percentage of sunshine—'

FROM CHILDHOOD some of Edith's happiest days had been spent in the country round Packwood (*overleaf*). Sometimes she took the train to Knowle and walked to the village across the fields. 'Haymaking was going on ... but the grass was still uncut in the church meadows. Being low-lying and marshy, there were numbers of flowers growing among the grasses .... Picked a great bunch of quaking grass ....'

ONE OF THE FEATURES that had most impressed her as a child about the beautifully kept gardens at Packwood House was the topiary intended to represent the Sermon on the Mount. Huge clipped yews represented, in order of size, Christ, His disciples, and the multitude. Edith loved to sketch here, perfectly relaxed among the ancient trees, while the birds sang in the garden around her, and the bees hummed like the honied voice of summer.

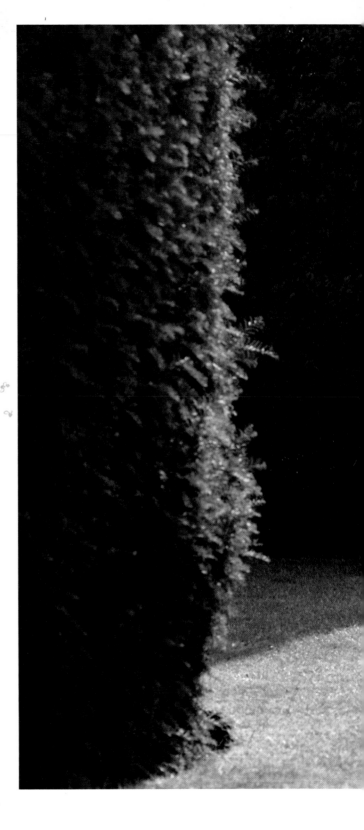

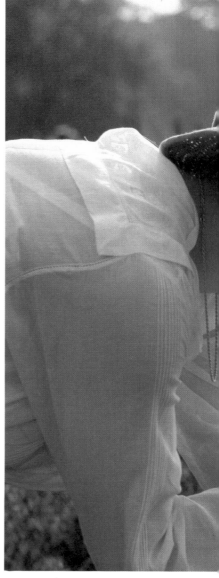

As Edith was cycling home from Baddesley, she heard a sudden yelp of pain. She dismounted at once and found a dog with its leg caught in a steel trap. She managed to calm the poor animal, and with some difficulty set it free. There came a shout from across the field, and the farmer appeared, striding towards her (*above left*). He told her in no uncertain terms to get off his land. He took

for granted his right to set traps for any strays that might molest his young animals. Edith went away with the dog in her arms. Much of her work, published through the National Council for Animals' Welfare and the RSPCA, was directed against this kind of thoughtless cruelty.

THE DOG ADOPTED EDITH with touching devotion and insisted on accompanying her everywhere, even on the train (*left*). She snatched a few minutes to admire the view while Winnie looked after him in the compartment.

THE CHANGING SEASONS at Packwood House were perfectly reflected in the brilliant borders, ornamental shrubs and trees. Edith could lose herself in the study of a single delicate flower (*above*).

THE FARMING LANDOWNER was still his own master, though city ways were beginning to invade the country. Communications were speeding up, though many goods manufactured in Birmingham were still distributed by an efficient network of canals, like the Stratford-upon-Avon canal in Warwickshire (*left*).

SOCIALLY, TIMES WERE CHANGING FAST, particularly for intelligent women. Liberty and equality—at last—brightened the horizon. It was exciting, but also disturbing to those who felt most involved. Edith hid her anxieties under a calm exterior: only sometimes, at night, they got the better of her. Then she longed for spiritual release, and yearning dreams of heaven would break in nightmare (*above*).

AUGUST THAT YEAR was to be one of the sunniest on record in England, but when Edith walked through the green and golden landscape to pick poppies in the cornfield (*overleaf*), 'a heavy shower early in the day had dashed most of the blooms'. She found 'quantities of Hare-bells on the field banks on the way home', and noted: 'Harvesting commenced.'

A LETTER FROM ERNEST SMITH, asking Edith to allow him to call on her, arrived too late: she had already made plans to holiday in Scotland. As the train carried her northwards (*left*), she looked out at the speeding view with mixed feelings. She regretted missing Ernest, but she repeated to herself that he was only a friend—a very much younger friend—and she tried to concentrate on her journey's end. She was going to stay in Callander, at the guest-house kept by Mrs Denovan Adam.

S COTLAND WAS NEVER DISAPPOINTING, even in dreary weather (*right*). If the colour of the landscape was blotted out by a storm, the sky was full of changing, racing cloud-shapes—armies, chariots, dragons—the stuff of legend and romance that held Edith spellbound.

B UT ERNEST followed his letter to Gowan Bank, where Winnie gave him Mrs Denovan Adam's address. Edith was astonished, on returning from a day trip to Oban, to find him waiting for her at the guest-house. Edith wrote: 'Cycled to Aberfoil by Lake of Menteith, and back by Loch Achray, Loch Katrine and Loch Vennachar.'

EDITH WAS ALWAYS HAPPY when she stayed with Mrs Denovan Adam, the widow of her most influential teacher. Many of his paintings hung in the house, and she never tired of looking at them, and talking over old times. She spent the days out of doors with Ernest. She always took her sketching things, and they wandered for miles over the heathery hills, settling to draw (*right*). whenever she found a plant or a view that particularly pleased her. 'Found numbers of beautiful little purple Heart's-ease growing on the short turf and came upon a big bog full of Grass-of-Parnassus, in the midst of the heather and Juniper bushes.'

NOW SHE FOUND THAT CONVERSATION can be better than silence (*above*), even when the birds are singing, and that two pairs of eyes somehow improve the view. Still she kept up her guard, for she was very afraid of being hurt, and she mistrusted her own power to captivate. But in her unguarded moments she was so attractive to Ernest, that he fell more and more in love with her.

ON THE LAST DAY OF THE HOLIDAYS, they walked across the hills to Lake Menteith. Edith noted that it was renowned for the number of large pike it contains. The walls of the little inn-parlour on the edge of the lake are hung around with fine, stuffed specimens in cases, that have been captured in its waters. They procured a boat, and rowed across to Inchmahome Priory (*opposite, above*).

THEY SPENT ALL DAY on the island (*opposite, below*). Edith was thrilled by the romantic ruins of the old priory, and recaptured the magic of childhood as they explored them together. She even indulged in a paddle—getting her skirt rather muddy in the process.

LOCH KATRINE in the Trossachs (*above*). Scenery like this drew Edith to Scotland again and again.

E NORMOUS SPANISH CHESTNUT TREES grew on the
island, reputedly planted by the monks. Edith
put up her easel and sat down to paint (*left*).
Ernest could not help feeling neglected, as if she
deliberately chose to sketch, rather than keep him
company on this last afternoon. He watched her for
a while, and then walked off by himself.

A S USUAL SHE HAD TAKEN REFUGE from a
situation that threatened to become too
intimate. Now she realized, too late, that she
had hurt him. Her reserve gave way at last to
overwhelming remorse, and grief that perhaps she
had spoilt her only chance of loving and being loved.

When he came back, he saw that she had been
crying. She simply turned to him, and he put his
arms round her (*above*). They stood together in the
ancient priory garden for a long time.

T HE SCOTTISH HOLIDAY WAS OVER. Edith had
to return to Birmingham and her teaching,
Ernest to London, and Lanteri's studio. They
took the train south together. Edith carried her
paintings, careful reproductions from that beloved
country, but her mind held grander images, of
mountains and lochs in all their wild splendour
(*overleaf*), a magnificent background to the miracle of
love.

Edith's visual memory had been so well trained, that when she was home again she could conjure up these scenes (*right*), and imagining Ernest beside her, his face and voice, the

BEYOND THE WOODED BECK (*left*), the hills sloped golden and green, the bracken turning to russet, the heather from pink to brown. Tucked away in the damp grass, wild flowers and brilliant fungi (*above*) revealed themselves to the observant eye. The hidden quality of these walks had always endeared them to Edith, but now she had discovered how sweet it was to share them with the man she loved.

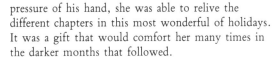

pressure of his hand, she was able to relive the different chapters in this most wonderful of holidays. It was a gift that would comfort her many times in the darker months that followed.

EDITH AND ERNEST were married by special licence at Chelsea Register Office. They lived in a flat (*left*) in Oakley Crescent. Ernest was now principal assistant to the Countess Feodora Gleichen, a fashionable sculptress whose studio was in St James's Palace.

THEY WERE NOT RICH, but that was unimportant (*above*). Ernest's work was exciting. All kinds of people came to the studio, from royalty whose busts would be sculpted in marble, to the most famous artists of the day.

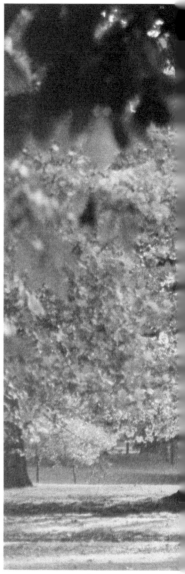

EDITH DID NOT WASTE TIME pining for the woods and fields of Warwickshire. During the day she worked—a book of children's poems with her illustrations, *Woodland Whisperings*, came out in the year of her marriage. But she loved to stroll out in the evening, with Ernest, or by herself, and discover unspoilt pockets of country in the teeming city.

THE TRODDEN GRASS and planned avenues of trees seemed more precious to her, because they grew in town. She loved to wander in the park, when the first lamps were lit, and most of London had hurried home for the night.

EDITH'S NEPHEW, ESMOND, came to stay with them in London (*above*). He was her brother Kenneth's oldest child. He enjoyed the visit, and it was fun to take him about—an excuse to go to the Tower and on the river—lighthearted excursions that had somehow slipped away, now she was married.

EDITH WAS BECOMING ESTABLISHED as a children's illustrator, and she should have felt proud and happy (*left*). But news of her father was not good—he was old, and ill. Besides this, there was a grief in her marriage: time passed, and still she had no children.

E SMOND SPENT SOME HAPPY TIMES with his aunts. He had picked blackberries with Winnie (*above*) and caught tadpoles with Edith.

A S ERNEST BECAME SUCCESSFUL, his work inevitably grew more demanding, and he was forced to spend long hours in the studio. Edith was proud of him, but she missed his company. She busied herself with her drawings, going out when the season was at its best to collect specimens (*above*).

F OR EVERY FAMILY IN ENGLAND, 1914 was a grim year. It was no longer possible to detach oneself from politics, when thick over Europe hung the clouds of war. Edith was lonely, and afraid. More often than not, her walks took her by the river (*right*). She would stand in a reverie, forgetting time and place, as the water flowed beneath her. It seemed that success, beauty, talent, pleasure—even love—all the worldly wealth that rocks the hearts of men—were sooner or later borne away on the flood.

SINCE HER MARRIAGE it had been difficult to keep in close contact with her family. Arthur Holden had died in 1913. Now Ernest was called up (*left*).

AFTER THE DEATH OF THEIR FATHER, bitter enmity had broken out between the brother directors over the running of the family firm. The case went to court, and involved both Edith and Evelyn, who were called as witnesses for Kenneth and Bernard respectively. Kenneth (*above*) lost his case. After this, the sisters were hardly on speaking terms.

RAINS had always been very much a part of Edith's life, links between the different events: the perfect holidays in Scotland and on Dartmoor, the momentous trips to London. Now there was one more journey to make to Warwickshire (*this page and overleaf*). She sat in the carriage with her *Nature Notes* open on her knee. It comforted her to remember those far off, uneventful days: 'The pale yellow fronds of Bracken looked very pretty in the wood, growing among the dark Bramble leaves. The road was quite yellow in places with fallen Elm leaves. One or two sharp frosts would strip the trees bare, although many of the leaves are still quite green.' The train sped towards Birmingham under its cloud of steam. Arriving at Olton station, Edith looked anxiously for someone to meet her. It was a melancholy occasion. After the collapse of his court case, Kenneth, already a sick man, had lost the will to live.

UNITED IN GRIEF, their grudges forgotten, the family assembled once more for Kenneth's funeral service. Afterwards Edith walked on her own in the churchyard (*above*). She could not help remembering all the sadness in his life: his unhappy marriage, his poor health, his bitter quarrel with his brother. His youthful promise had been wasted, and for him family reconciliation had come too late.

THE MORNING OF MARCH 15TH, 1920, dawned bright but chilly, with a threat of spring showers. Edith woke with a headache, but with typical stoicism she dressed and made breakfast, and planned her day. She was still looking pale when Ernest left for the studio, and he felt a little anxious about her, for she often complained of headaches. Presently she too left the flat, carrying her palette and easel, and her umbrella (*opposite above*).

SHE WENT TO KEW GARDENS, to finish work on a painting (*opposite below*). She loved sketching there. The great glasshouses were warm, and smelt damply of earth, their light was greenish and mysterious. She set up her easel among the exotic palms and tropical fruits, some of them taller than she was. She found them exciting after the tame English species she had patiently copied for so many years.

EVELYN HAD WRITTEN, inviting herself and Frank to Oakley Crescent for Easter. When Edith had finished her work, she posted a letter to her sister, telling her how much they were looking forward to the visit. While she was working she had forgotten her headache, but now it came back. She felt giddy and ill (*above*).

ERNEST WOULD NOT BE HOME until evening; probably he would be late. There seemed no point in returning to the flat, though her painting things weighed heavily on her arm. She walked along the river. The University crews were in training for the Boat Race (*right*), and she stood on the bank, watching them. The spring sun sparkled on the cold grass, and glittered on the water.

SHE FOUND A HANDSOME CHESTNUT growing close to the river (*left*). In this sheltered place its buds were more advanced than any she had seen that spring. A particularly beautiful cluster hung over the water. Edith drew out her umbrella, and balancing on a stump, reached forward to hook the spray with the handle. The slender branch resisted at first, and then, without warning, snapped. Edith lost her balance, and fell face down in the icy water. There was no one to help. As luck would have it, the Oxford and Cambridge boats collided, and the few people about were watching while the capsized boat was righted and its athletic crew struggled to safety. Nobody noticed the quiet little tragedy that was happening in the backwater.

WHEN ERNEST CAME HOME, very late, he found the flat empty, though the table was laid for supper. He assumed that Edith was out with friends, and went to bed exhausted. In the morning he hurried to the studio, expecting at least a message from her, but there was nothing. He returned to the flat to find a police constable waiting with the grim news. At the inquest (*above*), it was all too easy to reconstruct the tragedy. Edith had been found drowned. Her rolled umbrella and a spray of chestnut buds were floating beside her.

PART III

The Story of
The Country Diary
of an Edwardian Lady

As EDITH AND ERNEST hold hands in a cornfield near Wootton Grange they are closely followed
by Dirk Campbell (director), Paul Rudge (assistant cameraman) and
John Ward (Steadicam operator).

THE ADDER MAN stands in the rain outside Edith's hotel on Dartmoor (*above*). It was a triumph of planning, considering the wet spring of 1983, that only half a day was lost through the weather.

HERE DAFFODILS HAVE BEEN ARRANGED on the camera tripod (*above right*), to frame a shot of the two Ediths walking in the garden. They had been rehearsing a play at Gowan Bank. Edith Matthison, Edith's friend, was later to become a professional actress.

After Edith Holden's tragic death in 1920, her diary of *Nature Notes* remained in the family, and passed eventually to her great-niece, Rowena Stott, a young artist who recognized the quality of the painting, and felt that it deserved a wider public. In 1977 it was published by Webb & Bower with Michael Joseph, as *The Country Diary of an Edwardian Lady*, and soon it was breaking records, remaining on the *Sunday Times* best seller list for over three years, and number one on that list for longer than any other book.

Over two million copies in hardback have been sold all over the world. The following editions have been published:

UK and Commonwealth	Michael Joseph/Webb & Bower, 1977
USA	Holt, Rinehart & Winston, 1977
Sweden	Trevi, 1978
Germany	Friedrich W. Heye, 1979
Finland	Otava, 1979
Norway	J.W. Cappelens, 1979
Denmark	Lindhardt og Ringhof, 1979
Holland	Zomer & Keuning Boeken, 1979
Italy	Arnoldo Mondadori Editore, 1979
Spain	Editorial Blume, 1979
Japan	Sanrio, 1980
France	Editions Blume/Du Chêne, 1980
Catalan	Editorial Blume, 1980
Portugal	Editorial Blume, 1981

The paperback edition was first published by Sphere in 1982.

In association with Nigel French Enterprises Ltd, licenses have been granted to several leading manufacturers in Great Britain and abroad, in order to produce a wide variety of articles using the designs from the book. The twelve-part series produced by Central Independent Television plc, starring Pippa Guard as Edith Holden, sustains the remarkable interest captured by the *Diary*.

At first, the television treatment of 'the Edith Holden Story' seemed an impossibly difficult task. Her life, as well as her art, was in watercolours, and apart from its uncharacteristically dramatic end, it seemed altogether too simple, too delicate to bear the weight of a 'televised version'. However, it occurred to the producer, Patrick Gamble, that the year Edith Holden described in her *Nature Notes* might be related to the span of her life, its spring, summer, autumn and winter, and so form the basis of a biographical film.

He acquired the rights of the *Country Diary* in 1980. A deal was completed with Central Independent Television in June, 1982, with Brian Lewis as executive producer, for a dramatized twelve-part series of half-hour films, based on Edith Holden's *Diary* and the known facts about her life. Each part was to cover one calendar month, and filming was due to start early the next year.

With Patrick Gamble as producer, and Jane Ades associate producer, the director Dirk Campbell adapted the *Diary* for television and wrote the scripts with Elaine Feinstein. Locations were found—many of them, incredibly, in the very fields and lanes Edith had known and loved. The house and grounds of Parkfield, a large Edwardian house near Birmingham, were taken over for interiors and garden scenes.

Who was to play Edith? Clearly an actress able to carry a scene without the support of other players was needed, for Edith's was in many ways a solitary life. An introspective, sometimes difficult character had to be shown in a sympathetic light, yet remain true to the original. After lengthy auditions, producer and director agreed that Pippa Guard had the authority and the sensitivity to portray Edith.

Shooting of the film began on February 14th 1983, and continued, with breaks, until October 31st that year. It included about a hundred locations, in Warwickshire, Dartmoor and Scotland. As well as the main film unit, a natural history unit was employed in the making of the films. Its purpose was to collect diary material, but its work was complicated by intrusions from the twentieth century—the roar of a jet or diesel tractor overtaking bird song, for instance. Sometimes it was difficult to find the flowers Edith specified, but here the Warwickshire Nature Conservation Trust came to the rescue. So the *Diary* was used to link the episodes of the drama, through this nature film, and spoken extracts. But integrating the production of both units called for a high degree of skill, as well as imagination, and it was fortunate that the director was an experienced film editor.

A project of this size is in the end a question of team work. Its success depends on the performance of everyone involved in it, from the most gifted actor to the youngest member of the crew. Nor can the finished product correspond exactly with the original idea in the producer's mind, for films evolve in the making. But here there is something extra, a magical thread running through the drama—the voice of the real Edith, her delicate account of quiet days, her preoccupation with the beauty of small things. She painted sparrows, not birds of Paradise, and there is a sparrow in every English garden.

FILMING one of the autumn
Scottish scenes with Edith
and Ernest about to set off
across the loch in a small
rowing boat (*above*).

BACK IN THE STUDIO, editor
Bob Cook cuts the rushes
(*left*). 'Rushes' are rough
proofs of the day's filming.
Camera work is only part
of the highly complex
business of film making.

THE SCRUBBED SHELL OF THE KITCHEN at Parkfield
(*above*), a large Edwardian house used for the interior
scenes.

THE EDWARDIAN KITCHEN, as it appears in the film
(*right*). Subdued lighting casts convincing shadows,
and dulls the glare of white emulsion paint. It was
easy to furnish it correctly, but somebody
remembered to polish the handles on the stove, and
hang a voluminous petticoat to air.

Acknowledgements

The publishers would like to thank the following for permission to use illustrations in this book:

Local Studies Department, Birmingham Public Libraries 9; Central Independent Television Limited 31 (above), 34 (below), 38 (above), 41; Executors of Miss Doris Hamilton-Smith 20; Mr Esmond Holden 5; Miss Kaila Matthison 8; Mrs Vyvyan Palmer 23 (below); Mrs Hilda Rees 16 (below); Mrs Celia Stevens 12; Miss R. Rowena Stott 21 (above), 25, 26 (above and below left); Mrs Anne C. Williams 16 (above left, above centre and above right), 17.

Acknowledgement is also made to Ina Taylor for the use of original research material in this book.